CHOOSE YOUR OWN ADVENTURE®

Kids Love Reading
Choose Your Own Adventure®!

"I like the way you can choose the way
the story goes."
Beckett Kahn, age 7

"If you don't read this book, you'll get payback."
Amy Cook, age 8½

"I thought this book was funny.
I think younger and older kids will like it."
Tessa Jernigan, age 6½

"This is fun reading. Once you go in to have an
adventure, you may never come out."
Jude Fidel, age 7

Illustrated by: Keith Newton
Book design: Stacey Boyd, Big Eyedea Visual Design

For information regarding permission, write to:

CHOOSECO
P.O. Box 46
Waitsfield, Vermont 05673
www.cyoa.com

A DRAGONLARK BOOK

Publisher's Cataloging-In-Publication Data
Names: Montgomery, R. A. | Newton, Keith (Illustrator at Chooseco LLC), illustrator.
Title: Monsters of the deep / by R.A. Montgomery ; illustrated by: Keith Newton.
Other Titles: Choose your own adventure. Dragonlarks.
Description: Waitsfield, Vermont : Chooseco, [2010] | Summary: Your brother and sister are deep-sea explorers that have discovered the ancient Lost City of Atlantis. Now you get to explore the mysteries of the sea, and you have 8 possible endings to your story.
Identifiers: ISBN 1933390379 | ISBN 9781933390376
Subjects: LCSH: Underwater exploration—Juvenile fiction. | Atlantis (Legendary place)—Juvenile fiction. | CYAC: Underwater exploration—Fiction. | Atlantis (Legendary place)—Fiction. | LCGFT: Action and adventure fiction. | Choose-your-own stories.
Classification: LCC PZ7.M7684 Mo 2010 | DDC [Fic]—dc23

Published simultaneously in the United States and Canada

Printed in Malaysia

11 10 9 8 7 6 5 4 3 2

CHOOSE YOUR OWN ADVENTURE®

MONSTERS OF THE DEEP

BY R. A. MONTGOMERY

A DRAGONLARK BOOK

WATCH OUT!
THIS BOOK IS DIFFERENT
from every book you've ever read.

Do not read this book from the first page
through to the last page.
Instead, start on page 1 and read until you
come to your first choice. Then turn to the
page shown and see what happens.

When you come to the end of a story,
you can go back and start again.
Every choice leads to a new adventure.

Good luck!

You are preparing for your very first deep water dive!

Yes, you are scared. Who wouldn't be? After all, going down fifteen feet into the ocean—okay, it's really a shallow bay—is big time diving. Your siblings are famous for their deep, deep dives. They searched for the fabled Lost City of Atlantis, and they found it!

It's up to you to carry on the family tradition. So, mask on, snorkel in place, flippers flapping, you approach the salty ocean where monsters of the deep roam!

Hold on for a moment. It looks like rain.

Turn to the next page.

Big black clouds fill the sky. They look angry. But the sun is still shining. There is no rumbling of thunder. You don't spot any lightning either.

Just then, Avery and Lila, your two best friends, come up the beach carrying what looks like a picnic basket. They love adventures.

It's now or never!

If you decide to wait for your friends, turn to page 4.

If you decide to dive into the "deep," turn to page 6.

"Hey, over here!" you shout at your two friends.

"We're coming. Just hold your horses," Avery says. She has long black hair and is very smart.

"We brought a surprise," Lila adds. She has blond hair and loves to joke around. She is also very smart.

"I'm going diving," you say proudly.

"Not right now! Not yet," Avery yells. They start to hurry towards you.

Whammo! Zammo!

Thunder and lightning fill the sky. Rain pounds down on the beach sand. The sea becomes totally calm except for the rain plops.

You, Avery, and Lila get completely soaked. A bolt of lightning snarls from above. It heads straight at the three of you. Where can you go? What can you do?

Turn to page 14.

6

Sometimes you and your friends just don't agree. This is one of those moments. You decide to go for the deep right now!

You run (actually with flippers on you *clump, clump, clump*) down to the water.

Splash! Splash!

"Hey, wait for us!" Ave yells. Lila is running at top speed to the water.

You wait for a second or two and then jump in.

BONK!!!! You hit the sandy bottom. The water is only fourteen inches deep here. So much for the DEEP.

"We're coming!" Lila yells.

Your friends put on their diving gear. The three of you wade slowly into the warm, shallow water, and then dive down to explore.

Turn to page 9.

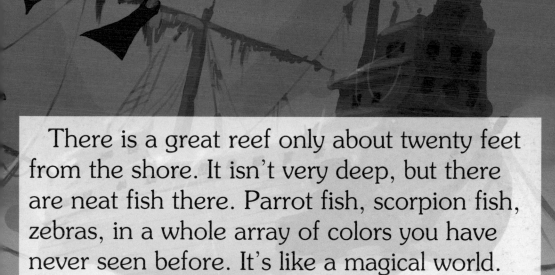

There is a great reef only about twenty feet from the shore. It isn't very deep, but there are neat fish there. Parrot fish, scorpion fish, zebras, in a whole array of colors you have never seen before. It's like a magical world.

Who's afraid of the deep now! No monsters here! Just beautiful, candy-colored fish.

Turn to page 63.

"Lie down! Lie down right now!" you shout. You throw yourself on the sand to make the smallest target for the lightning. Tall things like trees are dangerous to be near. Lightning likes to strike trees.

Something starts walking toward you across the beach, through the storm. It is a giant ghost crab. It gets closer and closer. It's as big as a car!

The ghost crab begins to dig in the sand with its many feet.

"Follow me," it says in human speech.

Avery and Lila look at you and then the crab.

"You said we need to get down and stay low," Ave says. "What do we have to lose?"

Turn to page 13.

"My name is Florence," says the ghost crab. "I'll help you get to where you're going!"

You like Florence. She is cheerful and calm, like your mom.

The crab digs a deep trench in the sand. Her face is down in the hole as she digs, and her legs are flying! You hear her sing a song while she works:

Scratch dig, scratch dig.
There goes the sand, there goes the sand.
Humans are fun but crabs are funner.
I've forgotten the rest, so that's a
bummer...

Suddenly Florence stops singing and digging. You peer over to see what's up.

Turn to page 15.

SNAP! CRACKLE! The lightning bolt hits a large tree on the edge of the beach. A limb breaks off and slams into the sand.

Lila shouts something. The thunder rumbles loud and fast, and you can't hear her.

If you decide to lie down in the sand to make yourself the smallest target for the lightning, turn to page 10.

If you make a mad dash for the small shack not too far away, turn to page 21.

Florence uncovered a golden whistle buried deep in the sand. It's a beauty. She holds it up and invites you to blow it.

RINNNGGGG! RINNGGGG! RINGGG! It's a really loud whistle.

Out of the ocean comes a leviathan—a big, big sea monster—from way in the deep. It is a giant blue whale. It spouts and blows. Its body is as long as a school bus.

Turn to page 17.

Its giant head comes to rest on the beach three or four feet from your small group.

"I'm Jonah. Tour guide of the ocean's deep. That's where all the mysteries lie. Ready?"

"I am," shouts Lila.

Turn to page 19.

You look at Jonah and Lila and Avery, wondering if you should let the Blue Whale guide you to the deep. Florence the crab climbs aboard the whale. There is a little sea craft with a window on the whale's side.

"That's an observation pod," Avery says. "See the oxygen tank on the side?"

"All aboard," Jonah shouts. "Time to go!"

Turn to the next page.

You, Avery, Lila, and Florence open the door of the pod and climb in. It's strapped to Jonah with material that looks like a sweat band for exercising. You hope it doesn't fall off!

Jonah backs up and swims out to sea. With a magnificent flip of his tail, you all shoot down into the deep. It is like an elevator ride, down, down, down you go.

"Hey, how deep are we going?" you ask.

"How deep do you want to go?" the crab asks.

So far on the trip you have seen sardines, anchovies, smelt, krill in the shallows, deeper still tuna and sharks—but what about the animals that live even deeper in the ocean?

If you want to stop at six hundred feet, turn to page 31.

If you want to go deeper, turn to page 37.

"Run for it!" you shout. Thunder *BOOMS* and lightning *CRACKS* very close by. You shiver. It's risky to run during a lightning storm. Have you made a mistake?

Heads down, the three of you dash across the wet sand. A wall of rain hides the little green shack with the white trim. Where did it go?

KABOOM! ZAMMO! More thunder. And the lightning is close.

Suddenly the wall of rain disappears and there stands the house—or at least what used to be a small green house.

Turn to the next page.

A sign outside says:
ENTRANCE TO THE GREAT DEEP.
DANGER.
You look at Ave and Lila to see what they think. They are really smart. But so are you. The Great Deep? The deepest part of the sea? The ocean floor is thirty thousand feet deeper than where you stand now. That's miles below you! It's too deep for humans.

Turn to page 24.

"Hey, guys, what do you think?" you ask, pointing at the sign.

"Sounds like fun," Lila says edging closer to the entrance to the GREAT DEEP.

"I think it means STAY OUT!" Avery says.

Just at that moment a giant tsunami wave crashes ashore. It sweeps the three of you up in its arms.

Turn to page 27.

The giant wave is as gentle as a newborn lamb. It deposits you, Lila, and Ave three hundred yards up the beach at a dairy bar. Going to the dairy bar is one of your most favorite things, next to Christmas, Halloween, school, your family, almost all sports—and of course, books!

"What'll it be?" Corny, the owner of the dairy bar asks. "It's on me today. Wow, that was one big wave. But you guys are fine, right?"

"Right," all three of you answer in chorus.

"Well, I'm waiting," Corny says.

"Vanilla with sparkles," Ave says.

"Strawberry and coconut and coffee, no sparkles," Lila replies.

"And you," Corny asks, smiling.

"Oh, I don't know. Maybe butter crunch."

So, you didn't go diving, but it has been a fabulous day!

The End

SPLASH! SPLASH!

Birds that look like arrows zoom into the water and grab fish from the column. Then they are gone. More fish come. It is a feeding frenzy. But the column keeps swirling and spinning. Most of the smelt survive the attack.

The sea becomes calm.

Josh reappears.

"Sorry about that. Just couldn't pass up a good meal," he says sheepishly. "It's our version of your fast food restaurants. No waiting. No hunting. Slash and grab, as they say."

"What's next?" Lila asks. Avery tries to shush her up.

"A giant squid," Josh says. "Follow me."

If you go with Josh to see the giant squid, turn to page 56.

If you go back to the Upper World, turn to page 60.

"Time for you three to return to the Upper World," she says. "Come again some day. Goodbye!"

With that, the three of you magically return to the beach where this adventure started. The sun is out. The sea is calm. What a day it has been.

The End

30

"Well, I hope you enjoy wherever you go next, down here in the Deep or back to the Upper World. You are always welcome here, brave explorers! Good luck!" The mermaid bows to you three. With a flip of her tail she swims away.

The End

"Tour stop: six hundred feet. Everybody get out and explore! Look out for sharks, swordfish, deep-swimming jellies, giant sunfish (two thousand pounds and up), and strange creatures. Also deep diving whales, submarines, underwater peoples, and very little sunlight."

Jonah likes to talk. Everyone on the tour knows that by now.

Turn to the next page.

"How do we breathe out there?" you ask.

"Simple. Just put on the deep-sea breathing helmet in the seat pocket in front of you. Then exit the pod into the ocean. *Bon voyage!*"

Turn to page 34.

Lila has her helmet on and is out the airlock door before you. It makes a huge *WHOOSH* sound behind her, double-locking the air inside. Avery and Florence the crab are ready.

Into the deep!

WOWZER!!!!

A great white shark cruises by, and it winks at you! You hope it's not a hungry wink.

Next, you spot two skates gliding by. They are beautiful. You like it down here.

Uh-oh! You think you see the long, long tentacles of a giant squid. Yikes! You, Avery, Lila, and Florence should scram back to the surface. Right NOW!

The End

"Quick, this way. Hide. The shadows are coming," voices from the coral forest sing to you. They part and show you a route deep into the coral.

But, isn't this the time to stand up, to be counted? To confront your fears? To banish the shadow once and for all? After all, how scary could it really be? Small things can make big shadows.

Turn to page 55.

"Deeper! Deeper!" the three of you shout.

"You asked for it," Jonah says.

He surfaces briefly for air, and then plunges into the abyss.

Down.....Down.....Down.

No light penetrates here. A tool in the pod shows you have dropped over two thousand feet, almost half a mile.

Turn to the next page.

It is getting colder by the minute in the pod. Florence huddles up close to Avery who kindly puts her arm around the ghost crab.

Deeper still! A giant shadow passes by. What was it?

The shadow moves on. No one but your friends and Jonah the whale are with you in this cold, dark world.

Turn to page 41.

Here and there are spots of glowing light.
Where is the light coming from?
Are they strange monster fish who live at great depths?
BUMP!!!!! BUMPPPPPP!
WHAT'S HAPPENING?
Suddenly Jonah reverses course and heads for the surface.
When you reach about the six hundred foot level you spy a friendly giant cuttlefish.
"Okay, everybody. The ride is over for the day. Hope you enjoyed it." Jonah doesn't sound too happy. Maybe he was scared too.
"Well, that's enough for now," you say to Ave and Lila and Florence. "Let's go build a magic sand castle."

The End

The mermaid is your choice and your two friends agree. Through the door into a magical world you go. You never in your wildest dreams expected this!

Fish dance by in spirals of colors. Many of these fish look like things you could only dream of: bear fish, giant eggplant fish, tiny spots of golden light dancing in huge clouds, winged creatures with human faces and silver and gold rings around their heads drift by as if on a summer breeze. Rainbows of light fill an enormous cavern. What is this amazing world?

"We shall all sing now!" the mermaid announces. She leads the three of you through halls of coral. The coral branches wave at you and laugh and giggle. "Welcome to our world," they say in a chorus of sweet voices.

Turn to page 44.

Finally you enter a round, sandy area. In two circles are whales, sharks, dolphins, tuna, octopus, rays, swordfish, and jellyfish, and creatures beyond belief.

A small catfish with big whiskers stands at a table. He raises a small coral fan. The fan squeaks in a happy tone.

"Okay! All ready?" the catfish conductor asks.

All the creatures nod.

Turn to page 47.

"What about us?" Lila asks. "We can play instruments."

The mermaid looks at the three of you, nods in agreement, and gets a mermaid friend to bring over two big conch shells and an old oil barrel from the upper world.

"Go for it," she says, nodding at the catfish conductor.

A baby blue whale winks at you. He looks like he is going to play a bass fiddle made out of live jellyfish and a living sea turtle.

Yikes! This is some world.

Turn to the next page.

The catfish conductor holds a baton made out of small swordfish swords. He raps it against the metal music stand in front of him. The concert begins.

You don't wait for the catfish to signal to you to play. You grab a conch shell and blow as hard as you can. Lila drums the oil barrel, and Avery plays the smaller conch shell. Lila runs up to the front.

Tap, tap! goes the catfish. Performers are supposed to stay in place!

Suddenly a big shadow from before slides past. Lots of the members of the orchestra make a run for it. What now?

If you decide to try to escape, turn to page 52.

If you decide to stay, turn to page 59.

"It's a school of fish. Sardines, probably. Could be smelt." Josh is smart. He knows a lot about the sea and its creatures.

"Why are they doing that?" Lila asks. She moves closer to the swirling mass.

"To protect themselves," Josh answers.

"From what?" Avery asks.

"From bigger fishes who want a quick meal," Josh says. He has a gleam in his eye. A hungry gleam. "From birds, too."

Just then a large tuna flashes into view and takes a huge bite out of the swirling bunch of fish.

Turn to page 28.

"Let's get out of here," you say to Avery and Lila. "I don't like this."

"Okay," Avery agrees, and heads for the coral forest.

The shadow glides over the area again, and more of the fishy orchestra leaves.

"This way," Lila says as she slips between two huge coral fans. They are pink and glow with a special power. They also speak in small voices.

"We will hide you. Follow the little golden fish. They will lead the way."

So, you, Avery, and Lila follow a school of tiny golden fish deep into the coral forest.

Turn to page 59.

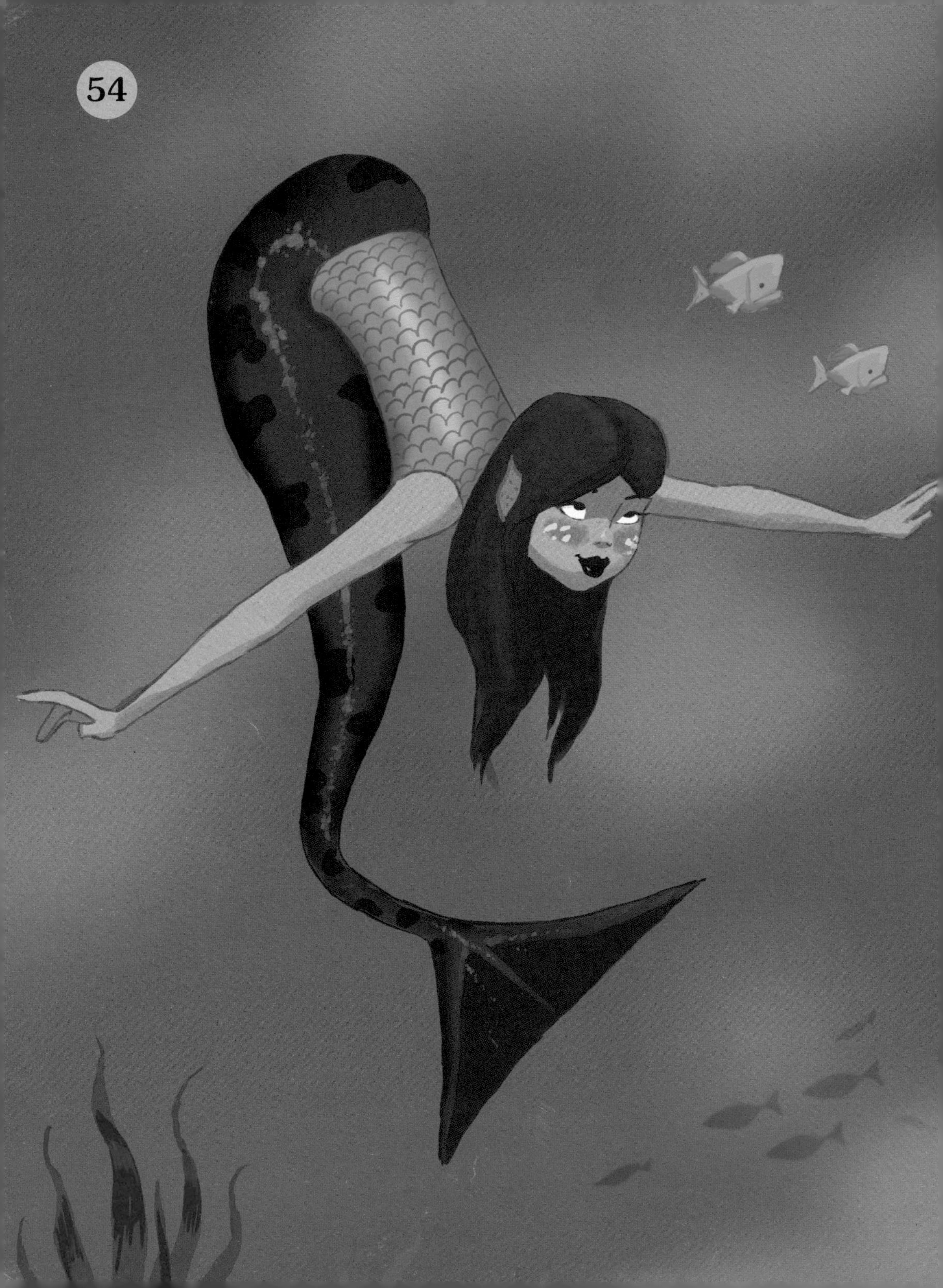

"NO!" you say. "I want to see what is making this shadow. I'm not scared!"

"Okay!" Avery and Lila say in chorus. "We're with you."

The two girls are already leading the way out of the coral forest. You follow them.

The orchestra is all gone. Only the catfish conductor and the lead mermaid remain.

"So, welcome back, brave ones. Want to know what the shadow was? It's gone."

"Yes!" you all cry. "Tell us!"

The mermaid looks at the three of you, smiles, and says, "The shadows were clouds in the sky in the Upper World. They mean no harm. Just clouds."

"Wow!" you say. "Clouds. I thought they were evil warriors come to do us all harm. I thought there was danger in those shadows."

Turn to page 30.

"Squid for me!" you say. You sound brave, but you are scared.

These creatures are big. They can be anywhere from thirty to sixty feet long. That's as big as your grandparents' Winnebago! They have eight arms and two huge tentacles. They fight whales. They are fierce predators.

Giant squid are found in deep, deep water in the oceans all over the world.

"This way," Josh says. He does a graceful, diving turn and heads to the deep.

On the way down you come across a giant sunfish, several whales, and an octopus or two. No sharks.

Turn to page 58.

"I don't like this. This is getting creepy," Lila says.

"I don't either," Ave adds.

But Josh leads you even deeper. The little sunlight down here is almost gone. Dark shadows and sudden movements frighten you.

"Josh, STOP! Stop now!" you yell.

But Josh is nowhere to be seen.

"What do we do now?" you ask your friends.

"I will help you," says a sweet voice. It is the voice of the mermaid. She emerges from the gloom.

Her smile, her glowing colors, her friendship are wonderful. She is magical.

Turn to page 29.

What monster of the deep is this shadow? you ask yourself. But you already know. It is the monster of the unknown. It is the monster where scary dreams hide. It is the monster of fear.

What shapes does this monster take in your mind? What dreams come up?

Now is the time to overcome the fear, destroy the questions of the unknown. Grasp the sword of courage and truth. Confront the shadow.

Fear lurks in dark corners, corners that can surprise you. You are brave. You are courageous. You know that you can overcome your fears.

Avery and Lila are also courageous people. How else could they be your friends? You three can trust each other.

Turn to page 36.

"I vote for going home—and NOW!" you say.
The girls agree. So, off you go.

Up. Up. Up. You never were very deep, but anything below the surface is deep to you.

Schools of small fish swim by. They seem to be having a party.

A kingfish and a sea bass look at you with big eyes. Then they just pass by.

Suddenly the color of the sea changes!

The sea changes from a dark blue to a bright green color.

It is warmer here, and the current is moving fast, much faster than the surrounding sea.

You are caught in this stream. What is it?

"Hey, we're in the Gulf Stream," Lila says. "It starts in the Gulf of Mexico and runs up the East Coast of the United States and then heads over to Europe. Wow!"

This river in the sea is one of many such currents. It is strong and powerful. You three can't get out of it. You are heading far from your beach and home.

What can you do?

Three dolphins appear.

"Want a ride? Just hop on."

The dolphins are kind and gentle. The three of you climb on their backs.

Before you know it you are back at your favorite old beach. You are safe and sound.

What a day. *That's enough of the deep for now,* you think.

The End

The barracuda looks at you, flashes its reddish teeth, grins and nods its head. It has a long, silver, shiny body. It is a beautiful fish.

"My name is Josh," he says. "Follow me!"

The barracuda is quite convincing.

So, the three of you follow the barracuda.

"This way," he says.

You all swim away from the world of the mermaid.

Two hammerhead sharks drift by, looking for a meal. All creatures search for meals. We do. Bugs do. Birds do. Mice do. Sharks do. But the sharks make you feel a little scared. You aren't used to the idea of being a meal!

Josh turns a sharp left.

Wow! You see a giant black and silver column spinning and spinning.

"What is it?" you cry.

Turn to page 51.

Uh-oh. Just when you think that, a nasty-faced Moray eel pokes its snout out of the coral defending its home. Fish swim away fast—so do you.

Turn to the next page.

As you swim after your friends, you spy what looks like a small metal door in the sand. It is about twenty feet down on the ocean floor. You have always been curious, and it has sometimes gotten you in trouble. Remember the time you tried to drive a tractor? *Crash! Smash!* Lucky you didn't get hurt. Remember when you put ping pong balls in the popcorn popper?

Lila and Ave swim over beside you.

"What's up?" Avery asks. Lila has already spotted the small metal door and swims down toward it.

"Look at that," you reply, pointing at the door.

Turn to page 67.

Who can resist a door without a lock?

Lila swims down and grabs the handle. She pulls, she tugs. You and Avery help.

SLURP!!!!

The door slides open. A mermaid swims out into the sea.

"They're real! I knew it! They're real!" Lila shouts.

The mermaid smiles at the three of you. She is about your size, with flowing hair, and green eyes, and scales!

"Welcome to the World of Wonder! We love visitors. Take this visitor's pass and come into our world." She hands you something orange and scratchy.

"Visitor's pass?" whispers Lila. "This is a starfish! She's confused."

Turn to the next page.

Just at that moment a seahorse swims by nodding and humming to himself. He is about the size of a big dog.

"How do we breathe down here?" you ask. You are always the practical one.

"Easy. Just like you do in the Upper World. You'll see. Follow me." She swipes her tail and vanishes into the World of Wonder.

Go on to the next page.

You realize that she's right—not only can you breathe, you can talk, too. This place must be magical. You and Lila take your masks off. But Avery looks worried. Maybe she'll keep hers on for a minute to be sure.

Florence the crab has returned to shore. No more adventure for her. Maybe she had the right idea.

Turn to the next page.

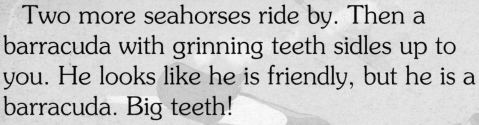

Two more seahorses ride by. Then a barracuda with grinning teeth sidles up to you. He looks like he is friendly, but he is a barracuda. Big teeth!

"I wouldn't follow her, if I were you," the barracuda says. "Trouble in there. Monsters. Follow me."

If you decide to follow the mermaid, turn to page 42.

If you decide to follow the barracuda, turn to page 62.

ABOUT THE ARTIST

Keith Newton began his art career in the theater as a set painter. Having talent and a strong desire to paint portraits, he moved to New York and studied fine art at the Art Students League. Keith has won numerous awards in art such as The Grumbacher Gold Medallion and Salmagundi Award for Pastel. He soon began illustrating and was hired by Disney Feature Animation where he worked on such films as *Pocahontas* and *Mulan* as a background artist. Keith also designed color models for sculptures at Disney Animal Kingdom and has animated commercials for Euro Disney. Today, Keith Newton freelances from his home and teaches entertainment illustration at The College for Creative Studies in Detroit. He is married and has two daughters.

ABOUT THE AUTHOR

R. A. Montgomery attended Hopkins Grammar School, Williston-Northampton School and Williams College where he graduated in 1958. He pursued graduate studies in Religion and Economics at Yale and NYU. Montgomery was an adventurer all his life, climbing mountains in the Himalaya, skiing throughout Europe and scuba-diving wherever he could. His interests included education, macro-economics, geo-politics, mythology, history, mystery novels and music. He wrote his first interactive book, *Journey Under the Sea,* in 1976 and published it under the series name *The Adventures of You.* A few years later Bantam Books bought this book and gave Montgomery a contract for five more, to inaugurate their new children's publishing division. Bantam renamed the series *Choose Your Own Adventure* and a publishing phenomenon was born. The series has sold more than 260 million copies in over 40 languages. He was married to the writer Shannon Gilligan. Montgomery died in November 2014, only two months after his last book was published.

For games, activities, and other fun stuff, or to write to Chooseco, visit us online at CYOA.com

Watch for these titles coming up in the

CHOOSE YOUR OWN ADVENTURE®

Dragonlarks® series for beginning readers

Your Grandparents Are Ninjas • Your Grandparents Are Spies • Your Grandparents Are Zombies!
• The Haunted House • Return to Haunted House • Your Very Own Robot Goes Cuckoo-Bananas!
• Your Very Own Robot • Gus vs. The Robot King • The Lake Monster Mystery • Dragon Day
• Search for the Dragon Queen • Your Purrr-fect Birthday • Princess Island
• Princess Perri and the Second Summer • Dino Lab • Caravan • Owl Tree • Fire!
• Indian Trail • Lost Dog! • Space Pup • Ghost Island • Sand Castle

 Purchase online at www.cyoa.com or ask your local bookseller